THE ANGEL
OF SANTO TOMAS

THE STORY OF
FE DEL MUNDO

BY TAMMY YEE

For further information, contact:
Tumblehome, Inc.
201 Newbury St, Suite 201
Boston, MA 02116
https://tumblehomebooks.org/

Library of Congress Control Number: 2021944781
ISBN 13: 978-1-943431-74-8
ISBN 10: 1-943431-74-4

Yee, Tammy / Angel of Santo Tomas / Tammy Yee — 1st ed
Book and illustrations by Tammy Yee

Printed in Taiwan
10 9 8 7 6 5 4 3 2

For Rosalina, who taught me patience
and unconditional love.

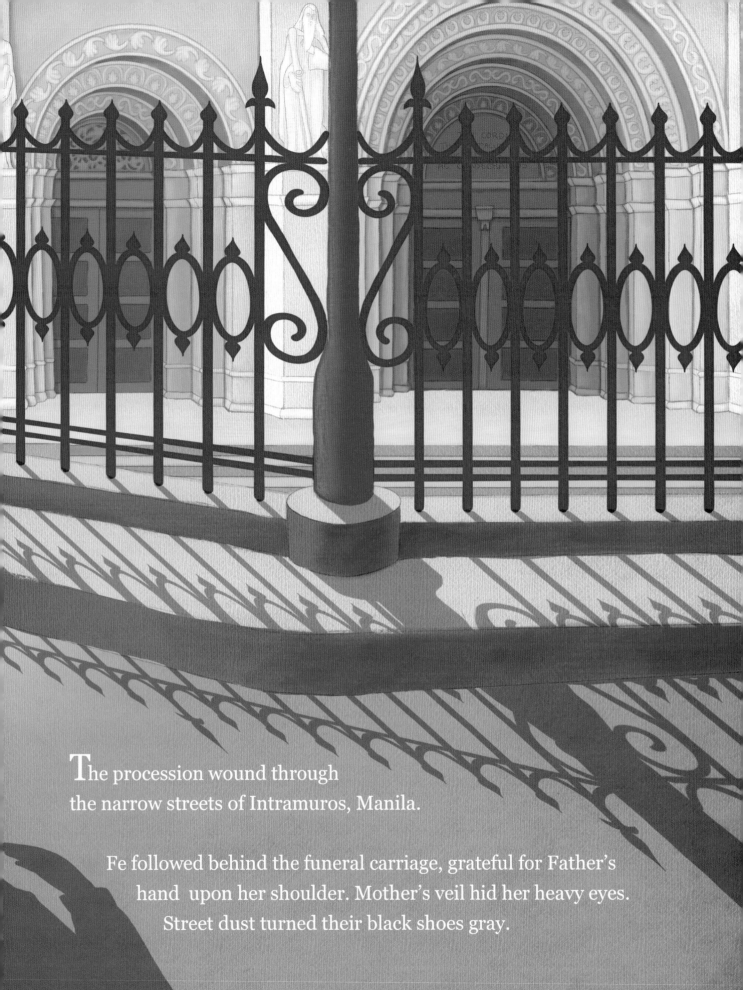

The procession wound through
the narrow streets of Intramuros, Manila.

Fe followed behind the funeral carriage, grateful for Father's
hand upon her shoulder. Mother's veil hid her heavy eyes.
Street dust turned their black shoes gray.

Back home, Fe lit a candle and opened her
sister's notebook. Between the pages, her sister
shared her dream of becoming a doctor.
Fe couldn't let her sister's dream die.
She vowed to take her place.

Three years later, Mother also passed away.
Fe's aunt welcomed Fe and her brother and sisters into her
home, where children ran up and down the grand staircase.

Fe's uncle was a well-respected doctor who invited her to assist him in his clinic and laboratory. She thrived under his guidance.

She was only fifteen years old when she entered the University of the Philippines.

Shy and barely five feet tall, she preferred books to spending time with friends. Speaking in class left her trembling with fear.

But her promise to her sister made her work hard. She graduated from medical school at the top of her class.

In 1936, she received a grant to study in the
United States. Arriving in Boston, Massachusetts,
she was sure there had been a mistake. She had been
assigned to a dormitory for men. Harvard hadn't realized
that Dr. Fe del Mundo was a woman.

Fe was allowed to stay. She became the first woman and first person of Asian descent to attend Harvard Medical School.

By early 1941, a great war raged across Europe and Asia.

Fe faced a choice. Should she stay in the United States where she was safe? Or return to the Philippines, where she was needed most?

Fe had made a promise to fulfill her sister's dream.
So, she returned home.

When babies who were born too early needed special care,
she kept them warm by nestling one basket inside another
and tucking heated bottles between them—
the world's first incubator.

On December 8, 1941, black clouds erupted over the Philippines. Soon, military forces entered the capital city of Manila and forced American, British, and other foreign civilians—men, women, and children—into a prison camp at the University of Santo Tomas.

Some children were left behind with maids and friends, without family to care for them. Three of those children were Fe's patients.

That night, Fe lay sleepless.

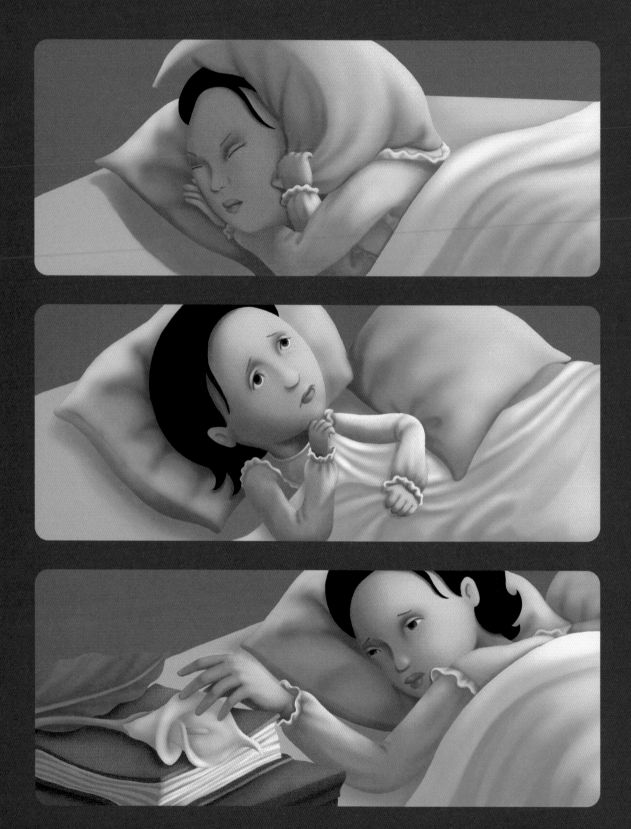

She could not rest while children suffered. Not only those who were left behind, but also those crowded behind the camp's arched gate, where food was growing scarce.

Fe rose early the next morning and asked the International Red Cross for help. Would they have space to house the children of Santo Tomas?

Next, she approached military officials. It was a risky plan, but she convinced them that removing the children from the sprawling, muddy camp would be best for everyone.

On January 10, 1942, Fe opened the Children's Home in the Red Cross building with seventeen children. Twelve more arrived the next day. Before long, the building was overcrowded.

Fe moved the home to the Sisters of the Holy Ghost College, which had a large playground. Also, it was closer to Santo Tomas, where the children's parents were interned. Soon the school bustled with 130 boys and girls.

The home grew to include pregnant women and mothers with infants. Staff provided health care and hot meals, and organized holiday celebrations, dancing lessons, and excursions to distract the children from the war. Most importantly, parents still interned in the prison camp were allowed visits with their children.

Fe became known as the Angel of Santo Tomas.

In February 1943, military authorities took over the Children's Home. Fe was forced to leave. Tearful internees honored her with an award for community service.

As the war closed in, the women and children were ordered back to the prison camp.

Finally, on February 3, 1945, American forces entered Santo Tomas and freed the remaining prisoners.

In the short time that she was in charge of the home, Fe had cared for 400 children. After the war, many wrote to thank her for her "loving heart and [her] Pied Piper way with children."

Years later, Fe opened the first pediatric hospital in the Philippines. The Angel of Santo Tomas had kept her promise—to her sister, and to the children of the Philippines.

*"She kept a little notebook where she wrote
that she wanted to take up medicine.
When she died, I decided to take her place."*
~Fe del Mundo

Gusto kong maging doktor

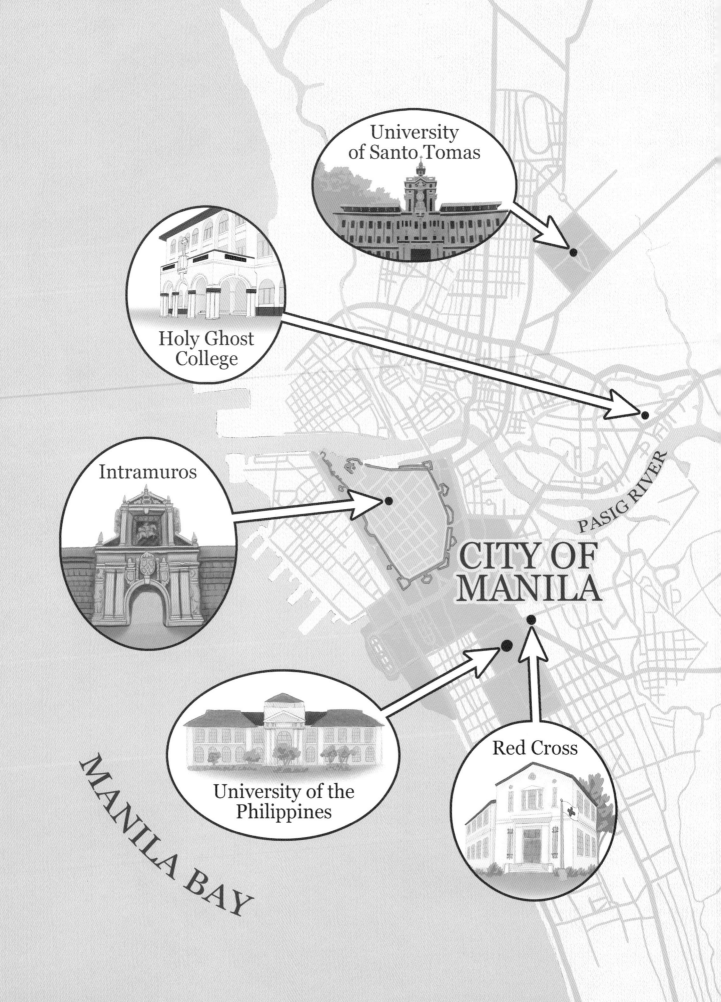

University
of Santo Tomas

Holy Ghost
College

Intramuros

CITY OF
MANILA

PASIG RIVER

Red Cross

University of the
Philippines

MANILA BAY

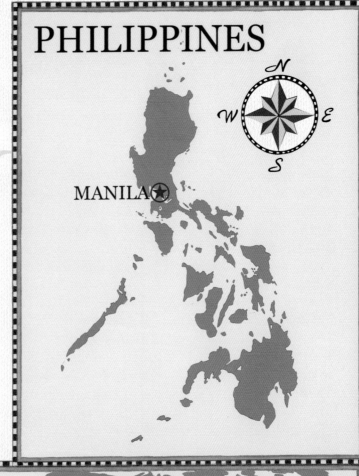

PHILIPPINES

MANILA ⋆

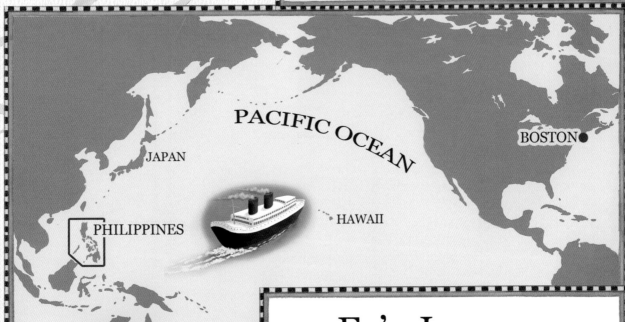

PACIFIC OCEAN

JAPAN

BOSTON ●

PHILIPPINES

HAWAII

Fe's Journey

Distance from Manila to Boston:
8,400 miles.

TIMELINE

"I saw how many children were not receiving medical attention and how many were dying." ~ Fe del Mundo

1911

November 27
Fe del Mundo is born in Intramuros, Manila, to Bernardo del Mundo and Paz Villanueva. She is the sixth of eight children.

Four of her siblings die in childhood. Among them is her sister Elisa, whose dream of becoming a doctor inspires Fe to study medicine.

1925
Mother, Paz Villanueva, dies shortly before Fe's high school graduation. Fe goes to live with her brother, Salvadore, and his family. Her aunt, Mercedes Hilario, and uncle, Dr. Jose Hilario, provide comfort and guidance.

1926
Fifteen-year-old Fe enters the University of the Philippines.

1939

September 1
World War II begins in Europe.

1941
Fe returns to the Philippines.

December 7
The United States enters the war.

1942

January 2
Military forces enter Manila. 5,000 American, British, and other foreign civilians and their families are forced into the University of Santo Tomas internment camp.

January 10
Fe opens the Children's Home.

1928
Graduates with an Associate in Arts degree and enters medical school. As a medical student she travels the countryside with a rural doctor. This experience inspires a lifelong dedication to preventing and treating illness in children and providing prenatal care to pregnant women.

1933
Graduates as valedictorian from the College of Medicine at the University of the Philippines. Awarded as "Most Outstanding Scholar in Medicine" by the Colegio Medico-Farmaceutico de Filipinas.

1936
Granted a research fellowship and becomes the first woman and Asian to attend Harvard Medical School. Studies at Columbia University, Mount Sinai Hospital, Massachusetts Institute of Technology, and Chicago's Billings Hospital. Receives a master's degree in bacteriology from Boston University.

1945

February 3
Santo Tomas liberated.

May 7
Germany surrenders in Rheims, France

September 2
Japan surrenders aboard the USS Missouri.

1944
Women and children return to the internment camp.

1943
Military officials take over the Children's Home. Fe becomes the director of Manila's Children's Hospital.

1947 Becomes the first Filipino certified by the American Board of Pediatrics as Board Diplomat.

1948 Travels to New York City as a delegate to the Fifth International Pediatric Congress, and studies other medical schools and hospitals. Returning to the Philippines, she opens the "Little Clinic" in her own home and dreams of building a world class children's hospital.

1957 With a loan and the sale of her home, she builds the Children's Memorial Hospital in Quezon City and dedicates it to the children of the Philippines.

1980 Becomes the first woman declared as a National Scientist of the Philippines.

2002 Children's Memorial Hospital is renamed the Fe Del Mundo Medical Center.

2008 Receives the Blessed Teresa of Calcutta Award from the AY Foundation.

2011 **August 6**
Dr. Fe del Mundo dies a few months before her 100th birthday. Until her death, she lived on the second floor of the hospital and continued to see patients well into her 90s.

"If you give the world the best that you can, the best will always come back to you." ~Fe del Mundo

1977 Receives the Ramon Magsaysay Award, Asia's equivalent of the Nobel Prize, for "her lifelong dedication as a physician extraordinary to needy Filipino children."

Receives Most Outstanding Pediatrician and Humanitarian Award at the 15th International Congress of Pediatrics.

1976 Edits and contributes to the Textbook of Pediatrics and Child Health.

1966 Receives the Elizabeth Blackwell Award, given by Hobart and William Smith Colleges to distinguished women "whose life exemplifies outstanding service to humanity."

Sources

Chua, Philip S., MD, FACS, FPCS. *An Icon Passes Away.* Far Eastern University, 2011. https://www.feu-alumni.com/announcements/fdm.htm

Del Mundo, Fe. Ramon Magsaysay Award Foundation, September 1977. https://www.rmaward.asia/awardees/del-mundo-fe/

Lim, Fides. *Woman of many firsts.* Philippine Center for Investigative Journalism, August 9, 2007. https://old.pcij.org/stories/woman-of-many-firsts/

Hilario-Libongco, Rose. *The family of Dr. Fe del Mundo remembers.* Philippine Daily Inquirer, October 30, 2011. https://lifestyle.inquirer.net/20163/the-family-of-dr-fe-del-mundo-remembers/

Acknowledgements

Special thanks to the Ramon Magsaysay Award Foundation for generously sharing Fe's biography, and to Dr. Ricardo Custodio for his unwavering support.

About The Author

Tammy Yee grew up in Honolulu, Hawaii, where she explored tide pools, caught crayfish in island streams, and collected monarch butterflies from crownflower trees to raise them into butterflies. After graduating from college, she cared for children as a pediatric nurse. Having her own children rekindled her love for picture books, so in 1994 she exchanged her stethoscope for a paintbrush and has been writing and illustrating ever since.